Old South Queensferry, Dalmeny and I

by John Hood

CW00499691

In this view of Hopetoun Road, South Queensferry, taken around 1917, Williamson Place is to the extreme right. Beyond Williamson Place, all the buildings seen here on the right-hand side of the road, as far as Plewlands House, have now been demolished. In contrast, the buildings opposite have largely survived, including the former Priory Church of St Mary of Mount Carmel. Originally a Carmelite friary, it was established in the fourteenth century on ground bequeathed by James Dundas of Dundas. For a period after the Reformation it served as a place of worship until, in 1633, the old parish church in the Vennel was opened. Now South Queensferry's oldest building, it has been used as an Episcopal church since 1890. Also in this area, at 8 Hopetoun Road, was the long-established and popular bakery run by David Ruthven. From his busy bakehouse and shop, David sold vast quantities of freshly baked bread, rolls, cakes and, above all, delicious meat pies, not only to a local clientele, but also to the sailors based at nearby Port Edgar.

© John Hood, 2007.

First published in the United Kingdom, 2007,
by Stenlake Publishing Ltd.
www.stenlake.co.uk
ISBN 9781840333954

The publishers regret that they cannot supply copies of any pictures featured in this book.

Although there has been a harbour at South Queensferry for over 300 years, the structure as it exists today dates mainly from the nineteenth century. It was then, in 1817, that local engineer Hugh Baird – whose work also included the design of the Union Canal – was commissioned by Queensferry Burgh Council to rebuild the harbour. Nowadays it is fairly peaceful, but in days gone by it was a bustling place and at its peak some 80 to 100 fishing boats operated out of the harbour. At one time there was a plentiful supply of young herring, or 'garvies', in the Forth around South Queensferry – enough to support a sizeable local fishing industry. In any one season, some 6,000 barrels of cured fish were exported and this product was also sold in the lanes around the harbour. It is said, unsurprisingly, that the vendors were easily identified by the strong smell of fish that came from them! In the mid-1800s, a new aroma was added to the area when a Mr Waddell opened his South Queensferry Gasworks. These works (the gasometer of which can be seen to extreme right) were taken over by the City of Edinburgh Gas Department in 1936.

INTRODUCTION

Until separated by successive local government reorganisations, all of the communities covered in this book were, for a long time, part of the old County of Linlithgow. By far the largest of these communities today is South Queensferry. Queensferry derives its name from the fact that the saintly Queen Margaret regularly crossed the Forth at this point, when travelling between Edinburgh and her court at Dunfermline. Around 1150 her great-grandson, Malcolm IV, gifted a piece of land and the 'right of ferry' to the monks of Dunfermline Abbey, an act that encouraged the growth of a small community. In 1363, Queensferry was raised to the status of a Burgh of Regality by David II. Finally, in 1641 it became 'ane free Burgh Royall'. Importantly (and much to the annoyance of neighbouring Linlithgow, which saw this enhanced status as being to the detriment of itself and its own harbour at Blackness), South Queensferry enjoyed special privileges, enabling it to develop strong trading links with the continent. These trading links allowed the burgh not only to indulge in a little shipbuilding, but also to become the home port for as many as twenty ships.

Although such trade had declined by the end of the 1700s, other industries such as fishing, soap-making and whisky distilling, had taken their place. South Queensferry's prosperity was then boosted in the late 1800s, when the Forth Rail Bridge was built to carry trains over the Queensferry Narrows. This bridge, considered one of the major engineering feats of the nineteenth century, put South Queensferry firmly on the tourist map and, to this day, still attracts many visitors to the area. In the early twentieth century, the economic prosperity of South Queensferry was again enhanced when, in 1917, a major naval base was opened at the former rail terminus at Port Edgar.

Surprisingly, until then, the burgh had expanded little beyond the old medieval boundaries, but the need for accommodation for the base personnel encouraged the construction of new housing. However, from the 1960s onwards, new housing developments were primarily intended for the influx of people keen to settle in South Queensferry. Some were attracted by the new hi-tech industries which had set-up in the area, others by its proximity to Edinburgh, although with the opening of the Forth Road Bridge in 1964, the ferries that had originally given the burgh its name disappeared.

The two nearby communities of Abercorn and Dalmeny initially developed around early religious settlements. They later became part of the estates of families such as the Hopes and Primroses, who built magnificent houses here on prominent sites overlooking the River Forth, and until well into the last century, village life revolved around the fortunes of these families, providing as they did, not only employment and housing, but also a range of social and recreational opportunities. For a brief period in the mid to late 1800s, both Abercorn and Dalmeny saw a dramatic increase in population and experienced new-found prosperity when extensive oil-bearing shale fields were discovered in and around the Lothian area. However, when the industry collapsed in the late 1920s many of the miners and their families moved out of the villages.

The final community covered in this book is the former seaport and village of Blackness. Located beside the once strategically important Blackness Castle, its early prosperity stemmed from the fact that it was the port for nearby Linlithgow. However, Blackness harbour (at one time the largest port in Scotland after Leith) lost much of its importance in 1680 when it was supplanted by Bo'ness. Thereafter Blackness suffered a steady decline. However, in the early 1900s it experienced something of a mini-revival when it became the favoured summer resort for Falkirk businessmen. At that time, many of the older properties around the harbour were pulled down or converted into holiday homes. Although Blackness continued to attract a steady stream of visitors throughout most of the last century, those that visit today do so largely to see the castle.

Acknowledgements

I would like to thank the following for their help during my research: Betty Archibald, who also contributed the photographs for the inside front cover and page 9, Pete Collinson, Rosemary Farrington, Robert Fleming Snr, Neil Garsitt, Janet Gooch, Rhona Lapsley, Mrs I. Law, Brian Lowden, James McLachlan, Mrs Manson, Valerie & James Munro, Tommy Nimmo, who also contributed the photograph for page 32, Mrs Pate, Bill & Irene Ross, Margo Smith, David Steel, Nan Wylie, who also contributed the photographs on pages 46 and 47, and Raymond Young. I would also particularly like to thank the Queensferry History Group for reading through and commenting on the manuscript.

Further Reading

The books listed below were used by the author during his research. None of them are available from Stenlake Publishing. Those interested in finding out more are advised to contact their local bookshop or reference library.

Collinson, Peter A., *The Royal Navy at Port Edgar*, Sinbad Productions, 2004.
Hendrie, William Fyfe, *Discovering West Lothian*, John Donald Publishers, 1986.
Queensferry History Group, *Doon the Ferry*, Queensferry History Group, 1991.
Queensferry History Group, *Back Doon the Ferry*,
    Queensferry History Group, 1992.
Williamson, May G., *The Origin of Street Names in South Queensferry and*
    Dalmeny, privately published, no date.

Although nowadays the hamlet of Society - which is situated two miles west of South Queensferry - barely registers on modern maps, in 1843 it was a thriving community which boasted, in addition to a cluster of stone-built houses at Easter Society, a private harbour and an inn. The latter was the turreted old Hopetoun Arms (seen here in the distance). Around the late 1800s the inn was closed and briefly became the residence of the Factor for Hopetoun estate. Now called Society House, it has for most of the last century been let out as a private residence. The Easter Society houses from left to centre of the photograph date from around 1774. These were built by James Hope, the third Earl of Hopetoun, for retired estate workers, but by the late 1970s were lying derelict and boarded up. However, without altering the external appearance of the houses, the late Graham Law (an award-winning architect of Law, Dunbar-Nasmith in Edinburgh) lovingly converted them over a four-year period into one large property, now called West Cottage.

This pre-1930s' aerial view shows South Queensferry from Galloway Pier to Hawes Pier. The former, which is to the left of picture, was a 900 feet long wooden pier which projected seawards from South Queensferry harbour's western wall. It was built in the late 1800s to enable passengers travelling on Galloway Saloon Steam Packet excursion steamers to embark and disembark at South Queensferry. The pier was demolished in 1925. The Hawes Pier (on the upper right) was South Queensferry's principal ferry terminus from 1810 until 1964 when, with the opening of the Forth Road Bridge, ferry services were withdrawn. In the bottom right is the former South Queensferry Goods Station. This station was opened in 1878 when the railway line was extended to Port Edgar. To the east of the goods station are some of the buildings of the former King George IV Whisky Distillery, owned by the Distillers Agency Limited. In 1969, when it was taken over by Sanderson of Leith, it was renamed VAT 69. The distillery closed in 1985.

This postcard, taken during the First World War by well-known local photographer, William Bain, shows staff at the North British Railway's South Queensferry Goods Station. This station, formerly called South Queensferry (Old) Station, was effectively the end of the line for much of the freight coming into South Queensferry; the remaining half mile of track which extended to Port Edgar had carried mostly passenger traffic for the rail ferry, prior to the opening of the Forth Rail Bridge. Under the Defence of the Realm Act (posters relating to which can be seen behind the staff in the photograph), the North British Railway Company lost control of (though not responsibility for) the track from the entrance to Shore Road into Port Edgar naval base. However, the line leading into the goods station was not affected and freight (including munitions and equipment destined for the war effort) continued to pass through the station. Although passenger services were finally withdrawn on 14 January 1929, this line was kept open until 1967, primarily to serve the whisky distillery.

From its opening in the late 1600s, Newhalls Inn (now better known as the Hawes Inn) was a popular stopping-off point for travellers using the historic Queensferry Passage to cross the River Forth. Its popularity dramatically increased when Linlithgowshire's first turnpike road was opened between Edinburgh and South Queensferry in 1751. Since then many thousands of visitors (mostly real, but some imaginary, like David Balfour and his devious Uncle Ebenezer in *Kidnapped*) have stayed at the inn. In 1905, when this photograph was taken, most of the visitors coming from Edinburgh to South Queensferry would have travelled in horse-drawn carriages. Within a few short years, however, these carriages had been replaced by the motor bus, although some considered that the eight-mile journey between the capital and South Queensferry would be better suited to trams. One of these was A. Horsburgh Campbell, the then Edinburgh Corporation Burgh Engineer, who stated in 1917 that 'the motor bus has its appropriate and economic place but Edinburgh to Queensferry … is not its proper province. This is, in fact, pre-eminently a tramway route'! This scheme was not, however, proceeded with.

In 1933 responsibility for the operation of the ferry service between North and South Queensferry transferred from the London North Eastern Railway Company to the Dumbarton shipbuilders, William Denny & Company. As part of the agreement, Denny undertook to introduce two modern car ferries, the *Queen Margaret* and the *Robert the Bruce*, onto the route. These ships, both launched from the Denny yard the following year, entered service shortly afterwards. Because of the increasing popularity of the route, these ferries were eventually joined by a further two – the *Mary Queen of Scots* in 1949, and the *Sir William Wallace* in 1955. Soon the four ferries were carrying more than two million passengers and 900,000 vehicles annually. In this photograph, a family is seen walking past a Ford Prefect and a Vauxhall Wyvern waiting to board the *Mary Queen of Scots*. Waiting times of an hour were eventually not uncommon at peak periods and motorists often preferred to take the long journey round by Kincardine Bridge to avoid queuing. The last ferry crossing took place on Friday, 4 September 1964, when after declaring the new Forth Road Bridge open Queen Elizabeth and Prince Phillip boarded the *Queen Margaret* at Hawes Pier. After ferry operations ceased, the ferries were sold to the British Transport Board.

The exact origins of South Queensferry's Burry Man custom are unclear. One suggestion is that this three-hundred-year-old tradition commemorates a shipwrecked sailor who, on coming ashore and lacking any clothes, saved his modesty by covering his body with the sticky burrs from the Lesser Burdock plant! But however the tradition may have begun, now every year on the day before the annual Ferry Fair, the Burry Man - almost entirely covered in burrs, wearing a floral crown, and carrying two floral staves - will make his way round the burgh. Customarily, this honour is confined to natives of South Queensferry. His two helpers, who are not required to dress up, are there to assist him in supporting the floral staves and help him sip the no doubt welcome nips of whisky supplied by each public house along his route.

Although South Queensferry had a more than sufficient number of small cafés and tearooms, some visitors were obviously content to bring a picnic – like Clare and Fergie, seen here on the foreshore with their tea and sandwiches while enjoying the fine views across the Forth. One popular place for day trippers was the area around Sealscraig, so called because of the seals which once sunned themselves here. For local children, going 'doon the shore' would have been a more active pursuit and might include swimming in and around the harbour, scouring the shell beds beyond the Hawes Pier for partans (crabs), or searching for 'sailors' soap' (green seaweed). Others would search the shore around Port Neuk (known locally as 'Port Nick') in the hope of finding some of the many 'lucky pennies' thrown out of trains passing over the rail bridge.

Opening of Bowling Green New Pavilion, South Queensferry.

Queensferry Bowling Club, formed in 1877, was a founding member of both the North Linlithgowshire Bowling League and the West Lothian Bowling Association. The club moved to its present site on the Back Braes around 1891 and some nine years later their new bowling pavilion was erected. This photograph, taken at the opening of the pavilion, shows members and their guests, complete with silverware. Since that time, the bowling pavilion has been replaced by a new clubhouse, an extension to which was opened in 1977.

On 1 October 1878, when the North British Railway's South Queensferry branch line was extended to Port Edgar, the existing stations at Newhalls and South Queensferry were closed and two new stations opened, one at Port Edgar and another alongside Catherine Terrace. The latter (shown here) was known as South Queensferry Halt and was primarily for the convenience of passengers terminating their journey at South Queensferry. The former was opened to enable passengers travelling northwards to connect with the ferry services operating between South and North Queensferry. In 1890, following the opening of the Forth Rail Bridge, passenger services were withdrawn and the two stations closed, although the line continued to be utilised for freight traffic. On 1 December 1919, however, the halt was temporarily reopened, proving particularly handy for sailors serving on the warships anchored in the Forth - from their disembarkation point at Hawes Pier, it was little more than a few minutes walk along Edinburgh Road and up McIver's Brae to the halt. Today, the former railway line forms part of a popular walkway and cycle path.

BRIDGE HOUSE, SOUTH QUEENSFERRY

The object of attention for the occupants of this early motor car (either a Hillman or Vauxhall) needs little imagination as, from their vantage point on Edinburgh Road alongside Bridge House, they had an excellent view of the Forth Rail Bridge! The mansion in the background has been known variously as Bridge House or the Royal Naval Sailors' Home. It was built in the late 1880s to serve as the office and private residence for the Forth Railway Company's Chief Engineer and, once work on the rail bridge was completed, it was vacated. However in 1895, following a local fund-raising campaign, the house was reopened as a shore-based home for officers and boys serving on the training ship, HMS *Caledonia*, and was renamed the Royal Naval Sailors' Home. It served this purpose until 1906, when the HMS *Caledonia* was withdrawn from service. For a few years at the beginning of the last century it was listed in Macdonald's Scottish Directory as one of three South Queensferry restaurants, then during the First World War it was commandeered for hospital use. Despite later being damaged in a fire, the external appearance of the house is little changed today, although in recent years it has been extended and converted into luxury flats.

In this photograph of South Queensferry High Street, taken just inside the old East Port entrance around 1910, John McFarlane's Anchor Bar and Cyclists Rest can be seen to the left. This inn was said to be the favoured watering hole for railway workers who stayed in Catherine Terrace at the top of McIver's Brae. Although many of the old eighteenth- and nineteenth-century buildings seen here on both sides of the High Street remain today, the narrow two-storey building beyond the steps leading up to East Terrace has gone. The terraces (East, Mid and West) were originally crude walkways built above a series of street-level cellars. However, around 1870, in order to meet pressing demands for more space, the cellars were converted into shops and the walkways above the cellars were upgraded to pavement standard. Among the many well-known businesses which have traded here over the years was that of local plumber and gasfitter, John Hinton, succeeded later by David Hinton.

Catherine Terrace comprised two blocks of brick-built terraced housing, hence its nickname of 'the brickies'. Erected on the Back Braes around 1883 by the newly formed Forth Bridge Rail Company for their workers, the houses had (as was common at the time) outside toilets and communal washhouses, one of which is seen here beside the railway line. Once work on the rail bridge was completed many of the workers moved out. However, the railway company retained control of the properties and thereafter made them available to local people. Unfortunately, as time passed and standards improved, the tenants became frustrated with the basic nature of the facilities and, from then until the eventual demolition of the houses, Queensferry Burgh Council fought a running battle on behalf of the tenants with the successors of the Forth Bridge Rail Company to have the properties improved.

South Queensferry, High Street.

In this late 1920s' photograph, taken looking west, some of the older properties on High Street can be seen. Although many of these still remain, the single-storey building with outside steps to the extreme right is now gone. This was Miss Jemima Morrison's Hole in the Wall public house. Next door to the public house was Gideon Fairlie (butcher) and, next again, the Caledonian Temperance Hotel (the building with three pillars). Still on the right, and just past the Pullars of Perth sign, is the old Queensferry Arms Hotel. Originally a coaching inn known as the Queens Arms, this hotel dates from the seventeenth century and is now the Orroco Pier Hotel. With its distinctive clock steeple, the A-listed former burgh tollbooth is the most prominent, and tallest, building on High Street. The steeple dates from 1720, when Henry Cunningham, MP for the Stirling Burghs, provided funding for a steeple, clock and bell. However, it is not known whether the steeple was actually a replacement for an earlier tower, or merely an extension to an existing one. Further alterations were made to the Tollbooth in 1894, when part of the structure to the east of the tower was demolished and Rosebery Hall erected in its place. The hall, which was seen as a welcome addition to the tollbooth, was presented to the burgh by Archibald Philip, fifth Earl of Rosebery, as a memorial to his wife. In 1888, to mark Queen Victoria's Golden Jubilee, the Burgh Council had the steeple clock replaced with the one seen here, which is still *in situ* today.

In this panoramic view of High Street, looking east from the Jubilee Clock Tower, some of South Queensferry's most historic properties can be seen. On the left-hand side of this narrow street, for example, can be seen the Caledonian Hotel, Fairlie's butcher shop, the Hole in the Wall public house, the Bank Buildings and the old Viewforth Hotel. On the right-hand side is Black Castle and, to the rear of Mid Terrace, the old parish church which dates from 1633. This was actually a 'burgh church', one of only twelve in Scotland, where the minister's stipend came out of the local rates. Black Castle (the building with the three dormer windows) is an A-listed building and dates from 1626. It is the oldest house in South Queensferry and was built for William Lowrie, a local shipowner. It is said that Lowrie's sister-in-law was one of fourteen women accused by the then parish minister, Ephraim Melville, of practising witchcraft, for which she was subsequently burnt at the stake at the Ferrymuir.

Around 1910, when this photograph was taken, the ground floor shops in the building on the extreme left were occupied by a licensed grocer and a milliner. By the 1920s, however, both premises had been taken over by the South Queensferry branch of the Hillwood Co-operative Society. The society originated at a meeting in a waiting room in Ratho Station in 1878! It later opened branches in several of the surrounding towns and villages, and operated mobile shops to serve more outlying areas. In 1965 the society was absorbed into the more powerful St Cuthbert's Co-operative Society which was, in turn, taken over in 1981 by Scotmid. On 18 August 1988 Scotmid opened a new store on the site of the former VAT 69 whisky distillery. On the extreme right of the photograph, can be seen A. Weir's tailors and clothiers shop on West Terrace. To the left of the photograph, on the corner of Gote Lane, is the Stag Head Hotel. Judging from the number of men standing outside it, this was a popular watering hole for the locals!

From the mid to late 1600s the narrow lanes and older houses around the harbour area were ideal in providing shelter for Covenanting rebels. Here they would lie low awaiting a favourable, or 'protestant', tide before embarking on ships bound for the Low Countries and safety. Although these houses had long since gone by the time this particular photograph was taken, the harbour area still has a 'crowded' look about it. Leading directly off the harbour head is Gote Lane, with Hillwood Place to its right. This property was built in 1910 on the site of an earlier house. It was named after Hillwood Co-operative Society, which once occupied the ground floor premises. In the centre of the picture is the malting sheds of the old Glenforth whisky distillery. Opened in 1828, it was South Queensferry's first distillery. The business was sold in 1863 to Kirkliston distillers, J. & R. Stewart. Although the malting sheds have now been demolished, the white building alongside, with the hanging oriel window, still stands and now forms part of the Orroco Pier Hotel.

The origins of this former United Presbyterian Church can be traced back to the late 1700s, when members of the established church broke away in protest at the appointment of a new minister. Then, following a meeting held in Echland (later known as Echline) on 13 November 1775, the congregation successfully petitioned the Burgher Presbytery in Edinburgh for a minister of their own choosing. Their new church – St Andrew's – was opened in September of the following year at Church Place. This church was eventually replaced in February 1894 by the one seen here on The Loan. In 1900, when the congregation merged with the United Free Church of Scotland, the church was renamed the South Queensferry United Free Church. There was a further change of name – to South Queensferry St Andrew's – on 1 November 1929, when the church joined the Church of Scotland. Yet another name change occurred when, in March 1956, on their merger with Queensferry Old Parish Church, the church became Queensferry Parish Church. Since this photograph was taken, a church hall has been built onto the south side of the church, opening in March 1973.

In 1876 the Dalmeny School Board opened a new single-storey school and schoolhouse on Burgess Road. This was to replace an earlier seventeenth-century parochial school which had been located alongside the old parish churchyard. Due to increasing school rolls, the new school had to be extended on several occasions, but eventually it was replaced in the 1960s by a new primary school built further along Burgess Road. Today the original 1876 school building (in the centre of this photograph) is used as a primary school annexe and nursery, and its several extensions as a community centre. In front of the school is Burgess Park, which was once owned by successive Earls of Rosebery who allowed local inhabitants to use it for recreational purposes. For many years it was the venue for local football matches and, in recent years, has also been used for some of the annual Ferry Fair festivities. All the properties to the left of photograph have survived.

Doubtless it was the plethora of bakers and tearooms in South Queensferry at the turn of the last century that caused the senders of this postcard to remark that their appetites were 'appalling' and that they were considering staying for at least a month! On this short stretch of Hopetoun Road alone, in addition to Thomas Thomson's long-established baker and confectioners in Hopetoun Place, there were also two tearooms. The first (also in Hopetoun Place) was most probably John McLean's Hopetoun café and tearoom which, as an added service, also offered to 'stable' cycles. The second tearoom was located on the opposite side of the street, where the 'Cyclists Rest' sign is hanging.

In this further view of Hopetoun Road, also taken around 1917, most of the photograph is taken up by the frontage of Williamson Place. This was built as a speculative development in the late 1880s, when the railway line was extended to Port Edgar, and comprised a suite of shops at ground level with apartments above. Here, some of the many shops which ran in an unbroken sequence along the entire length of Williamson Place can be seen, including John Donaldson & Son (painters), J. Mitchell's tearooms and 'Aggie' Beveridge's sweetie shop and tearoom. Aggie, who was in business here for about thirty years, sold a mouth-watering range of sweets, including penny Vantas which were extremely popular with local children. The presence of policemen in this photograph can be explained by the fact that the double-gabled building next to Williamson Place was in fact the old police station.

In this view of the West End at Shore Road, taken around 1915 and looking east, the single-storey Queensferry Infants School can be seen on the right. This school, known locally as the 'wee school', was built in 1866 on ground gifted by the Dundas family and their friends 'in grateful and affectionate memory of Mrs Mary Shaw' who had been a nurse at Dundas Castle for fifty years. Today, the site is occupied by South Queensferry Library. On the left-hand side of the street, almost directly opposite the school, is white-washed Priory Cottage which at one time was occupied by 'Jockie' Wilson, a well-known local carter. The open ground alongside the cottage was where South Queensferry's first cinema eventually stood. This cinema, which was in existence throughout the 1930s and 1940s, was run by Robert Daybell, who also had a boarding house near Hawes Pier. For a period after the cinema closed, the building was used to store furniture, but it has since been demolished.

CLARK PLACE

SOUTH QUEENSFERRY.

The construction of a new ferry terminal at nearby Port Edgar in the late 1870s seems to have been the catalyst for a spate of house building around South Queensferry's West End. Within the decade, tenements such as Clark Place (shown here) and Springwell Terrace were built by speculators and let out by private landlords. It is thought that some of the homes in Clark Place (for example, those with bay windows) may have been for slightly more affluent tenants, but within about twenty years of their construction the local council was being bombarded with a constant stream of complaints about the houses. Often these related to poor sanitary conditions and the need for modernisation - the houses had shared outside toilets (situated on the landings) and, although washhouses were provided, there were no drying greens. On 24 April 1949 a fierce fire ripped through the neighbouring whisky distillery and, while the blaze was being fought, occupants of Clark Place were required to empty their houses of all furniture and store it temporarily in nearby Rosebery Hall until they could return.

Almost as soon as construction of the new naval base at Rosyth was completed, work began on a subsidiary base at Port Edgar. Built on the site of the former rail ferry terminus, it was officially opened in December 1917. Known as HMS Columbine, it was used as a shore-based destroyer depot. It played a vital role during the First World War, but in 1929, with the bulk of the British fleet having been transferred to the Cromarty Firth, Port Edgar was put up for sale. One proposal, put forward by a consortium of trawler owners operating out of Leith, Newhaven and Granton, was to provide berthing for up to 500 trawlers at Port Edgar. However, ultimately the base remained unsold and still in the control of the Admiralty. This was later to prove fortuitous for, with the outbreak of the Second World War in 1939, the naval base was again required – on this occasion as a training school for minesweeper crews. It continued to be used for this purpose until its closure in October 1975 (except for a brief period in 1943 when it was used to train tank landing craft crews for the D-Day landings).

Although the naval base at Port Edgar was not officially opened until December 1917, by the spring of 1916 the first of the (largely 'M' class) destroyers to be based there were already using the partially completed pens. These destroyers or, to be exact, torpedo boat destroyers were designed to form a 'perimeter screen' around large warships and merchant ships to protect them from torpedo attack. As such, the ships were extremely fast, and armed with 4.7″ guns fore and aft, in addition to a complement of three or four torpedoes mounted on their upper decks. The pens at Port Edgar, when fully operational, could accommodate up to 66 of these destroyers, including the newer 'V' and 'W' class. In his excellent booklet on the Port Edgar naval base, Pete Collinson recounts that, because of the similarity of appearance of these destroyers, it was not uncommon for sailors, having returned to their ship after a night out, to wake up the following morning and find themselves on the wrong ship!

The pressure on the destroyer pens at Port Edgar was substantially increased following a decision taken in April 1918 to move the 150 warships that comprised the Grand Fleet from Scapa Flow to the River Forth. Although various anchorages were found for these vessels, the destroyer flotillas inevitably were berthed alongside the already crowded pens at Port Edgar. Following the closure of the naval base in 1929, all of the pens (with the exception of 'E' pen) were dismantled. However during the Second World War, when the base was reopened, a new jetty was constructed alongside 'E' pen and the 6th Minesweeping Flotilla was tied up here. After the Second World War a variety of ships used Port Edgar. These included minelayers, motor minesweepers (known as 'Mickey Mouses') and fishery protection vessels (known as the 'Fish Squadron'). In the early 1960s, the latter became caught up in the 'Cod Wars' conflict between Britain and Iceland.

Between 1918 and 1927, these red brick Royal Naval barracks on Shore Road were home to several hundred sailors serving in the Port Edgar naval base. Despite the large numbers of naval personnel, security was provided by officers drafted in from the London Metropolitan Police – such as the officer seen here near the entrance to the barracks. The barracks were temporarily vacated in the late 1920s when the naval base closed. However, during the Second World War, when the base was reopened, part of the barracks were converted for hospital use; on 8 March 1938, a new 200-bed military hospital, complete with operating theatre, had been opened within the barracks buildings. From then until a few years prior to the closure of the hospital on 27 April 1950, it dealt with an average of 4,000 admissions a year. In the 1960s, following an expansion in the role of the naval base, the barracks were restored to their former use until their closure in 1975. The barracks buildings still stand today and are now used by the National Museum of Scotland to store items in their collection.

In this view of Shore Road, taken on 24 December 1927, we see the red brick frontage of the Port Edgar Naval Base Officers' Club. This club, known as the Flotilla (or 'Flot') Club, was built around 1920 for social and recreational activities. After the final closure of the naval base in 1975, the building was used by Lothian Regional Council for a number of years, again for social and recreational activities. However, by the 1990s it was in a poor state of repair and around 1994 was sold to Castle Rock Housing Association for conversion into a sheltered complex for senior citizens. As the building is a B-listed structure, the work (which was undertaken at a cost of approximately £2 million) was carried out in collaboration with Historic Scotland. Work on the conversion lasted approximately eighteen months and during this time the exterior was stone-cleaned and the interior substantially altered. The official opening of the sheltered complex took place on 14 August 1996.

In the early 1890s Admiralty plans to establish Sick Quarters in or around South Queensferry, for men and boys onboard the training ship HMS *Caledonia*, were accelerated by an outbreak of scarlet fever. To resolve this issue, two acres of ground at Lower Butlaw were leased from the Earl of Hopetoun and a temporary galvanised-iron hospital was built at a cost of £500. This hospital, seen here shortly after opening, was extended in 1903, when additional land was acquired at Upper Butlaw on which to build a permanent hospital. By 1905 the first of the new, permanent, hospital buildings of the then-named Royal Naval Hospital South Queensferry was complete. In the run up to the First World War, the hospital was upgraded in order to provide hospital facilities for the new naval base at nearby Port Edgar. Its first real test came in early June 1916 when, shortly after the Battle of Jutland, wounded sailors from Admiral Beatty's Battlecruiser Fleet were taken on board the hospital ship *Plassy* (which was anchored off South Queensferry) before being transferred to Butlaw. The hospital closed in 1927.

In the early 1930s, some of the Nissan huts on the Royal Naval Hospital site at Butlaw were temporarily acquired from the Admiralty by Councillor Andrew Murray, Chairman of Leith Market Hall Unemployed Club, for conversion into a holiday camp for families of the unemployed. For two weeks in the summer these families, coming mostly from the West of Scotland, participated in a range of recreational and social activities, even planting vegetables and rearing poultry. In 1933 the former Voluntary Aid Detachment building at Upper Butlaw was also pressed into service, on this occasion by a Glasgow charity, to provide similar holidays for schoolgirls. However, all of this ceased in 1939 when Port Edgar naval base was reopened during the Second World War and the site was once again required by the Admiralty. At that time, and until the eventual closure of the base in 1975, the buildings at Butlaw were used solely for training purposes.

This little Romanesque church at Abercorn was built on the site of the earlier monastery of Aebercurnig, which was founded *c.* AD 675 by followers of St Ninian. The earliest portion of the church dates from the late eleventh century and comprises little more than a nave and chancel. In the seventeenth century, however, burial aisles and vaults were built onto the south wall by both the Duddingston and Dalyell families. The most striking internal feature of the church is the Hopetoun Gallery. This large gallery, which overlooks the pulpit, was designed by Sir William Bruce, architect of Hopetoun House, for the Hope family. The church has some eleventh- and twelfth-century 'hog backed' sculptured stones, which are now kept in the Session House Museum at the church. There are also some eighteenth- and nineteenth-century gravestones for workers on the Hopetoun estate. Some of these have been engraved to indicate the person's occupation thus, for example, a gravestone for a gardener has an engraving of a tree, spade and pruning hook, while another for a baker has three small loaves and a rolling pin.

65628 J.V.

Construction of Midhope Castle began in the late 1500s on the orders of Alexander Drummond of Midhope. When complete, it was little more than a five-storey square tower house. The four-storey extension, seen here on the right, was added in the seventeenth century by George Livingstone, third Earl of Linlithgow. As hereditary keepers of Linlithgow Palace, the Livingstone family actually resided in the palace itself, only using Midhope as their country seat. In 1678 Midhope Castle became the property of the Hope family, who lived there until the far grander Hopetoun House was completed in 1699. By the time this photograph was taken in 1909, Midhope Castle had long been converted into flats to house the families of workers employed on Hopetoun estate. Although still occupied as late as 1929, it lay empty for a period in the mid 1930s, before being used during the Second World War by local Home Guard and ARP units. Today, Midhope Castle is presently disused, although restoration work carried out during the last twenty years has protected it from further deterioration.

This idyllic looking row of stone-built cottages is situated within the Hopetoun estate at Upper Parkhead, just north of the western entrance to Hopetoun House. Built in 1879 to provide accommodation for some of the estate workers, the cottages have changed little over the years – the exception being that the middle two doors have now been converted into windows and consequently their small triangular porch roofs have gone. A few hundred yards further down the road, at Lower Parkhead, lies a similar row of cottages dating from 1881. The boys in this photograph would most likely have attended the then newly opened Abercorn Public School at White Quarries, whose 'dominie' was the redoubtable Christopher Dawson. At the time this was an 'all boys' school – girls attended a local 'girls only' school which had been established by one of the Countesses of Hopetoun. The girls' school closed down c. 1903 and thereafter they also attended Abercorn Public School. The school has now been converted for use as office accommodation.

When extensive shale oil deposits were first discovered in the West Lothian area in the late 1850s, entrepreneurs such as James 'Paraffin' Young formed companies to extensively work them. These companies also created small townships in the vicinity of their mines, in order to provide accommodation for the workers and their families. The Newton (as it is commonly known) was one such community. It was developed around 1870 by the Oakbank Oil Company for employees working in their nearby White Quarries Shale Mine. The entrance to the mine was situated alongside Abercorn Public School, which many of the children seen here on Main Street would have attended. Further along the street, on the left-hand side, is the nineteenth-century Duddingston Arms public house which would probably have been well patronised by the miners. The village store also stood in Main Street. Although the shale mining industry was initially prosperous, by the early 1920s it was in such serious decline that a distress fund was set up by the government of the day to relieve the plight of shale field miners.

The Primrose family acquired the estate of Barnbougle and Dalmeny in 1662. They resided at Barnbougle Castle on the estate until 1817, when Dalmeny House was built. It is said that the castle had once been owned by a crusader, Sir Roger de Mowbray, who, along with his faithful hound, died fighting in the Holy Land. According to local legend, the spirit of the hound returned to Barnbougle Castle, where it was said to roam nearby at the aptly named Hound Point searching for its master! In the early 1800s, the castle fell into disrepair. It was then that Sir Archibald Primrose, the fourth Earl of Rosebery, commissioned English architect, William Wilkins, to build Dalmeny House – Scotland's first Tudor Gothic Revival mansion. Although still a private residence, Dalmeny House has been open to the public during the summer months since 1981, when visitors have the opportunity to admire its fine collection of paintings and porcelain. Barnbougle Castle, which lay in ruins for a period, has now been restored.

Dalmeny Station, South Queensferry.

Until the opening of the Forth Rail Bridge, passengers alighting at Dalmeny village would have done so at the old Dalmeny Station. Thereafter, that station was closed and a new one built slightly to its west. This new station, now known simply as Dalmeny, was initially known as Forth Bridge Station. The first person of any note to use the new station was the then Prince of Wales, who passed through on his way to open the new Forth Rail Bridge. On that occasion, the Royal Train stopped in the middle of the bridge to allow the Prince to drive home the last rivet. In 1939, during the Second World War, the appearance of a German fighter plane in the skies above South Queensferry caused the Dalmeny stationmaster to halt the Edinburgh to Fife train. As an added precaution, passengers were instructed to leave the train and shelter in the station buildings. Afterwards, when the 'all clear' signal was given, the train was allowed to continue on its way. Much to the passengers' dismay, once the train was on the bridge further enemy planes were spotted in the skies above. However, their target was not the train or the bridge, but warships anchored nearby.

These houses, known as Rosshill Terrace, were erected in Dalmeny's Station Road in the late 1800s for railway workers, when connecting lines were laid to Dalmeny to enable trains to run on the newly built Forth Rail Bridge. Comprising two blocks of red brick terraced houses, they were more commodious than the little cottages in nearby Dalmeny village. Unsurprisingly they were eventually let out to villagers who were in need of a larger house. Typically, each house comprised a dining room, kitchen, scullery and toilet at ground level, and either two or three small bedrooms upstairs. In the distance are some of the Dalmeny Station buildings, including the two-storey stone-built former administrative centre of the Forth Bridge Railway Company. For a period this was used as a control centre for monitoring all the surveillance cameras installed in railway stations throughout Lothian Region. Today it has been converted into office accommodation.

In this early view of Main Street, Dalmeny, we can see some of the nineteenth-century properties that line both sides of the village green. Those on the left include the two properties that jointly comprised the village school and schoolhouse. Although the school roll was generally modest, the influx of shale oil miners and their families in the latter half of the 1800s temporarily caused the school roll to climb to 200. The school was closed in 1967 when a new primary school was opened in nearby Carlowrie Crescent. At that time the single-storey school building was converted into a village hall, while the three-storey building alongside it was demolished, thus opening up the view to the twelfth-century St Cuthbert's Church, which can just be seen to the rear of the school. The rows of terraced cottages on the right were mainly occupied by workers employed on the Rosebery estate, but also included the old smithy (the cottage with the tall chimney stack on its front elevation) and the local joinery.

This lodge house was one of nine on the Dalmeny estate. It is located to the north west of Dalmeny village and is today little changed in external appearance. It is known as Chapel Gate, perhaps because of the style of its front facing windows, but more likely because of its proximity to St Cuthbert's Church, which is considered to be one of the finest surviving Romanesque churches in Scotland. Within the church can be found the historic Rosebery Aisle, where members of the Rosebery family and their guests worshipped. The family burial vault, where several generations of Roseberys are buried, is in the graveyard. Being close to the entrance to Dalmeny Station, the lodge keeper and his family would no doubt have witnessed the coming and going of many important visitors to Dalmeny House, as they passed through the wooden gate alongside the lodge. These visitors included Queen Victoria and William Ewart Gladstone.

DALMENY F.C.

The opening of the new Dalmeny Primary School in the late 1960s brought with it opportunities for recreation and sports within the precincts of the village, since the old school was converted into a community hall and the new school had a football pitch. However, this came too late for Dalmeny F.C., seen here around 1928. The lack of a football pitch and therefore home game advantages would no doubt have badly affected this local club. It may also account for the fact that, unlike other local teams such as South Queensferry's Bellstane Birds, Dalmeny F.C. don't appear in any standard histories of the junior game. Active in the 1920s, during its lifetime the team is likely to have played in either the Linlithgowshire or Edinburgh & District junior football leagues. It may also have competed for the Rosebery Cup, which was presented by Lord Rosebery for member clubs of the Edinburgh & District Junior Football Association. Long since defunct, one of the few facts known about Dalmeny F.C. is that they played in primrose and pink, the racing colours of Lord Rosebery whose horses won the Derby in 1894, 1895 and 1905.

Until 1680 the bustling harbour at Blackness (which served as nearby Linlithgow's seaport or 'haven') was second only in importance to Leith. Its trading privileges had been conferred in 1389 by Robert II to his 'dear burgh' of Linlithgow. In 1680, when the Blackness Custom House facility was transferred to Bo'ness, the Linlithgow magistrates fought back and succeeded in having it returned to Blackness. In an effort to ensure that the facility remained there, the magistrates had the Custom House renovated and offered the Freedom of Linlithgow to all shipowners who agreed to set up business in Blackness. It was to no avail - in 1713 the Custom House facility was once again transferred to Bo'ness. When the *New Statistical Account of Scotland* was published in 1845, Blackness harbour was said to be in ruins and the former Custom House had been converted to accommodate summer sea bathers.

In the early twentieth century Blackness experienced something of a revival when it became a favoured summer holiday destination for Falkirk businessmen, some of whom built holiday homes there. By the mid 1920s Blackness had earned the name 'the Brighton of Falkirk' and was attracting a monthly average of 3,000 visitors over the summer. However, not all these visitors were from Falkirk. Generations of Bo'ness children would at one time walk from the shore, or 'crookies', in Bo'ness and along the foreshore path (part of which is in the centre of the photograph) to Blackness, picking brambles on the way, and perhaps stopping to look at the cows on Low Valley Farm (which can be seen on the right). On arrival in Blackness they would play on one of the beaches or visit the castle. One Bo'ness resident recalls that these excursions usually also included a visit to Fleming's shop in the Square to buy cinnamon balls, pear drops or clove rock, before beginning the walk back to Bo'ness.

The charabanc in this 1920s view of the Square at Blackness is parked alongside a three-storey property known as the Guildry. This building was originally built as a tobacco warehouse for goods waiting to be shipped abroad, at a time when Blackness was a busy seaport. It was later converted into housing, but by the 1960s had unfortunately become something of a local eyesore and was demolished by West Lothian County Council. Shortly afterwards, the present-day Guildry was built on the same site. In the distance, between the Guildry and the western gable of Sea Yetts, is Blackness Castle. Built around 1440 by Sir George Crichton, then Sheriff of Linlithgow, this castle (built in the shape of a ship) was at one time one of the four most important strongholds in Scotland. For a period it served as a state prison and later as an army central ammunition depot. In 1912, after many years of neglect, the garrison was withdrawn from the castle and the castle was placed in the hands of the Ministry of Works, and designated an Ancient Monument. For the duration of the First World War, however, the castle was temporarily garrisoned once again. It has since undergone a restoration programme and many of the alterations made to it (particularly when it was converted into an ammunition depot) have been reversed.

Between 1870 and 1874 a considerable sum of money was spent converting Blackness Castle into a central ammunition depot for the army in Scotland. To create this new facility, a powder magazine and storage space for heavy artillery and munitions was constructed within the castle. In addition a light iron-girder pier and 1,000 feet long sea wall was constructed on the seaward side of the castle to facilitate the loading and unloading of ammunition. Two further buildings were erected within the castle grounds to house officers and soldiers guarding the depot. The two-storey Barracks Block seen here was 124 feet long and could accommodate up to thirty soldiers. Although its external appearance has changed little since construction, over the years the interior has been altered to enable it to be used, firstly, as a YMCA hostel and, more recently, as a Historic Scotland shop.

Around 1912 the garrison at Blackness Castle consisted of one lieutenant, one sergeant and 25 men. In this view, taken around that time, some soldiers in kilts and plumed headgear can be seen marching to the village where on Sundays they would attend Blackness Mission Church. This church (known locally as the 'garrison church') was built in 1901, primarily for sailors serving on the Royal Navy ships anchored in the Forth. Initially, it was no more than an outpost of St Catherine's Scottish Episcopal Church in Bo'ness, although eventually it was raised as a full charge and renamed St Ninian's (Episcopal) Church. In later years it was put on the market and bought by the Church of Scotland.

In this early view of Blackness village, looking west from Blackness Castle, the building nearest the camera on the left is the small single-storey village school. This one-teacher school was built around 1857 at the behest of Captain James Hope of Carriden for the education of local children and comprised one classroom and an adjoining schoolhouse. Despite its size, the school had a separate entrance for both boys and girls. It was vacated in 1904, at which time a new school was opened nearby. Thereafter, the old school was used as a church and, latterly, as a branch library, before being sold to its present owners in 1968. The two-storey building behind the school is Turnhouse. Built in 1908 for the Braes family, it was both a house and a dairy. Standing in front of Turnhouse is the whitewashed single-storey dairy byre which was only recently demolished. To the right of the photograph is East Bay. Although a popular spot for picnickers, the favoured beach was in fact Back Bay (also known as Castle Beach), which was accessed through the kissing gate to the east of Blackness Castle.

One of the most distinctive buildings in Blackness is the three-storey Art Nouveau Nosirrom Terrace. It was built around 1912 by Falkirk builder and bookmaker John Morrison – in fact, the word Nosirrom is simply Morrison spelt backwards! It is thought to have been the work of Bo'ness architect Matthew Steele, who was said to be much influenced by his old teacher, Charles Rennie Mackintosh. This particular project was one of several 'social housing' programmes Steele undertook for West Lothian County Council. Other examples of his craftsmanship can still be found in Bo'ness, such as the restored Hippodrome Cinema and Bo'ness Masonic Hall. Externally, Nosirrom Terrace has altered little in appearance over the years. The portion on the left is actually owned by the grandson of the original builder. Also largely unchanged in appearance is the two-storey Sea Yetts, which was built onto the western gable end of the terrace at a later date.